THE
PINK
BOX

POEMS

YESENIA
MONTILLA

Willow Books, a division of **AQUARIUS PRESS**

Detroit, Michigan

THE PINK BOX

Editor: Randall Horton
Cover design: Amber N. Tatum

ISBN 978-0-9961390-7-6
LCCN 2015950229

EMERGING POETS & WRITERS SERIES

WILLOW BOOKS, a division of AQUARIUS PRESS
PO Box 23096
Detroit, MI 48223

Printed in the United States of America

This book is dedicated to Maritza Montilla,
Janette Figueroa & Eric De Silva

The purpose of life is to be defeated by greater & greater things.
—Rainer Maria Rilke

Contents

III. The Otherworld

The Pink Box
for Nina & Monica

I asked how she got so skinny & she said she digged so
deep, pulled out all her poems from inside the pink box.

I wanted to ask her where she bought this box. Did she keep it
near the Darwish poems? Where did it live this pink box?

I started to imagine how it had been made. By women
in the rainforest who specialized in this type of pink box?

Or some sentient being that felt its way through the world,
creating this space and navigating within the box.

I dreamed of calling her & asking, she'd say*, Girl I made it
all by myself out of cardamom leaves & saffron strings, that pink box.*

I never called, only continued dreaming, of owning a space
where all my poems would live & recline when tired, a pink box

like the kind she had, the kind that makes a poet's teeth rattle like a
Christmas bell, announcing the news, the availability of a spacious pink box

in the world, better than an Easter basket or a red wheelbarrow.
Instead a bona fide perfectly symmetrical poem-holding pink box.

I wonder, will I call it Jessie or Yesenia? I need it, else I'll have to continue
carrying my poems around like a baby on a sling, in the absence of a pink box.

I. The Wilderness

So I was born with sore
limbs & pink flesh, rare like an orchid
untamed
I grew into myself like an unopened calla
with a strong green stem.

Raise

for my mother & my father

I.
I was forged
from my mother's
ache for her
homeland
& my father's
oversimplification
of the word home.
She confused
the concepts,
my mother:
home & homeland
are not the same.
One is supposed
to offer fruit
while the other
is the root
of the tree.
I was raised
like a crystal chandelier
high above four
tenement buildings.
Like a weed too
I was forced
to grow in between
sidewalk cracks.
A kind of wilderness
where I was expected
to be both lioness &
gazelle.

Their meeting
I think of today
while the snow
covers my city,
I think they met
in Central Park

ate sardines
out of a can.
I think my dad
wore a short afro,
my mother wore
a dress just right
for her young girl hips.
They discussed what
the heat allowed.
They did not stop
to think of the things
white people think of:
money, education,
bedtime stories.
Instead they just laid
themselves down
their love covered
their ears
their eyes
their mouths too
so there could be
no space
for questioning.
Can I be like them?
Were they brave
or foolish?

II.
On my way to work
I am lugging
a work bag
heavy as hell
crimson pink
like Brooke Shields' lips
in that movie with the
beach & the kiss

& I am swaying
as the subway pulls
in & out of every station
holding myself
together thinking
where a stroller
would fit.
Would I breast feed
in this chaos?
Can I afford the private
school with the farm,
the eco-friendly ways?
Can I teach my child
to be colorblind?
Teach others to love?
& my thoughts
lull like seagulls
flying over the Hudson
laughing at New Jersey,
that is when I know
I ain't ever gonna raise
a brown baby
in this damn city.

The Patron Saint of Lost Grandmothers

I pray to the saint
of lost abuelitas. But how
can I pray for something
I never lost. See your face
on the side of project
buildings but never once
have felt you take up space
in my home & my bones.

What do you look like?

I look at the hunch of my
mother's shoulders,
the weight of her not
knowing you sits
at the nape of her neck.
I want to rub the sorrow.
Let it become light as lychee
juice, or grated coconut, grow,
fly, bury itself & ghost away.

What do you sound like?

Basalt is how I envision
your skin today, grandmother.
Each pore a consequence
of too much longing—
a hole into which
I dream of pressing my
slender fingers, clogging
the desperate need you might
have of holding my mother
to your body.

Would you hold me too?

How do I find you, abuelita?
Should I dive off the tip
of the Florida Keys, my white
dress a phantom atop rough
waters.

Should I touch
snouts of sharks & lull them
into aiding my journey, abuelita?

Search for you in the Cuban countryside?
Speak the lost *Taíno* words my
past remembers?

Oh Patron Saint, offer the words
so I can sing her forward.

Dendrology

The Summer of '77 I learned
the Spanish phrase: pelo malo
when my aunt announced
I'd never be loved by a white man
con ese pelo malo. I loved my hair,
the way it frizzed around the edges
of my face & stood there like a woman
waiting to be asked to dance a slow bolero
a jumpin' rumba. I was three years old
didn't know much of love then.
The orange tree that stood in my aunt's yard
became my first lover. I would wrestle with
its tender branches, hoist my small frame
around its tubby brown trunk thick as a liana
or a man's waist. I wonder now if every lover
in my bed in some ways is a representation
of that orange tree & those words I heard
in that Miami heat about the way love
can be so damn fickle that the texture of my hair
would wilt a pink crotched man, make him
recoil from my locks. Today, I still do
have a fondness for trees, all of them
with their deep roots & their heartwood.
The alamedas holding rows of them, singing,
shading my unruly hair, reminding me that once
I was told there would never be an arboretum
in my future. That I'd never have the gift of choices:
bonsai, white birch, redwood—

Numbers

Eight, she didn't know
     she would grow up to be on welfare
         In the regime's school system,
     she took gymnastics & dance,
         part of a well-rounded Cuban education

Nine, she didn't know
     she would come to America
         Her skin was darker than the others
     she had no idea this would
         pose a problem at P.S. 144

Ten, she didn't know
     she would fall in love   have a baby
         two years after that
another baby & another &   again
     when much older, one more

Eleven, she didn't know
     she would forget her mother's name
         or how her mother looked on the runway
            when the plane took flight & carried

her to this place where bubble gum
     & Elvis were king

Twelve, she knew that she had landed
         in a foreign place where Spanish
            could not be spoken on the subway
it would upset the   "honkies"
     & she wanted so much to be accepted

Sixteen, she tried to play by the rules
She became a "busy-bee" & a "team-player" &
couldn't help but notice that her father was a "drunk"
her stepmother a "drug-addict", her brother a "fag"

Thirty,   fourth baby   the
      birth certificate read "unknown"
           next to the father's name. By then
           she was too unraveled to notice that
                Fidel was still in power & the price
                      of the American dream had risen too high

La Llorona Part I

She is known as La Llorona
but I know her only as mother.
As a child, I would watch her
apply red lipstick, curl her bangs
reach for the blackest dress in the
smallest closet, kiss my forehead as
she left me in the small apartment to
skip down the street toward
the funeral of: Alejandro el bodegero,
Tatiana la hija de fulana de tal, Bonito
de boy hit by a drunk driver *right there,*
en la esquina imagine that. From our
five-floor walk up I would hear her
howling. Sometimes she'd sit quietly
in the back row & peer at the back
of the mourning widow's head
her gray hair like the moon &
my mother, on all fours howling, as though
the grief carried in each follicle was her baby.

I remember the first funeral I attended with
La Llorona, her arrival was received with tears
the kind so salty the grains prevent the wetness
from descending down the cheek, instead
they'd slip off the side of the face, wet the ears,
the congregation deaf from crying.

Last night I dreamt I died & La Llorona entered
the parlor where my limp body waited for her
to howl. When all four winds gather at a crossroads,
waiting to raise you up, they dance with you
a hard bolero before dropping you off at home.

La Llorona Part II

It started with a birth & a death.
She was born
the day love died & since
has associated death with responsibility.

She was, after that day, known as La Llorona &
Saturdays when the funeral home was full
you could hear all the children
stop playing at jacks or marbles & yell
as she walked by *La Llorona, La Llorona, como
Llora, como Llora*

The children's cries would bring solace
to the grieving & the sighs that escaped
from the funeral parlor were thick enough to anchor
the gone & keep them in the realm of the living.

She would enter the space & begin to wail,
the sound hitting the air becoming humid & syrupy.
Some say her sound was like that of a river
whose current stirred boats that carried the dead.

After My Mother Is Diagnosed with Cancer They Throw Her a Séance

I drank Vodka straight at twenty

so grown   I knew everything then

        The bells chimed   each clink

like a baby's cries   I dreamt of milk

        I sneered at the sight of them

they believed so readily in the   otherworld

        Oshun   Yemaya

            The lights dimmed like dusk

in the tiny two bedroom apartment

        I leaned against the wall   giggled over the scene

then   a wild animal   squeezing my heart as though it were

        a   plum   I

woke surrounded by them   the ladies in their colors:

                    blood   vines   veins

pinning my arms down

        to hold back the wicked   pink lipped snake

reaching for their necks

& my mother, sitting on a backless chair
holding her stomach. She told me later
I felt the cancer leaving—

Playing Chicken with My Mother

Some hens are terrible creatures,
they barely feel the egg being ripped
from underneath their warm
feathered bodies & even still don't
miss that one egg when there
is still one or two left in the chicken
coop to roll their breasts on.

The day my mother said *here take*
your brother, he is yours now I was
14 years old, I cared for him
like a doll; whispered things
in his ear while casually
leaving him too close
to the bed's edge.
He was plastic with a soul

& yet, just the other day
he knocked on my door
begging: *momma let me in*
but it was time for me to leave
that door closed. Let him run
to his real momma keep him
at bay, force her to accept
that some chicks are not pampered
equally, indulged on fervently,
& this trespass is a debt
that should be paid.

Hummingbird
for Junot Diaz

I do hope you get this message
because it is five hundred
& eighteen years
in the making.
I wonder if the Tainos
knew of you.
That you would come
to us one day
like a hummingbird.

I knew you before you arrived.
You read comic books,
stored them under your bed:
the Silver Surfer at it again
leaving rings of ambition around our earth...

I knew you before you arrived.
Immigrant boy   Outcast
Wings like the hummingbird   Traveler
A copper kettle in a sea of stainless steel pots.

Ode to a Dominican Breakfast

Keep your pancakes, french toast, eggs
benedict, your muffins & scones

Keep your waffles & four types of syrup
the way your eggs scramble but never sizzle

Nothing more scrumptious than mangu con queso frito

The other day I wore a white dress
with a wide skirt & a red sash

I danced merengue barefoot on my stoop. I kissed the
Dominican flag, once for each time I remembered a Taino word

yuca, batata, tanama, ocama, yautia, cacique, juracan,
every bite on the plate, every morsel like a bachata tune

This can all be yours, get off the long lines at the brunch spot
Forget the grits & cheesy okra. Ring my doorbell

Five ingredients: Olive oil, onions, plantain, white cheese & flour

& I ain't even tell you about Morir Soñando—

They Say
        for Ayiti

They say the last sound heard before dying
is the voices of your children, & if you do not have
children you hear the voices of your parents, & if
you do not have parents then you hear the voices
in the row houses next door, their singing
an introduction to how graceful death can be.
But what happens when the burying is done while still living?
When the earth like a spoiled child given too many candies smiles
its rotten teeth at you & swallows you whole. You lose

your footing. What do you remember then? I remember
the cement blocks like sandpaper tearing at blue skin—

I've talked to the dead, they say what you remember
last is how the dirt feels invading the lungs, crushed
glass on cement before the settling, before the glass buries
itself in its new home, before it cuts space in the place
right there where heels touch, make paths, plant provisions,
berries even grow wild there.

I remember my last breath escaping through my nose
instead of my mouth, sore & strained from screaming
god—

The last sound I heard were the feral dogs
tearing into my leg; it shook & rattled
trying to find its way back to me.

The last thing I saw was my rusty old teapot by my head.
I swear it looked brand new, double handled
like a man with his hands in his pockets.
I swear it was red, I swear it even whistled.

Hispañiola

My grandmother
has a native look to her.
Her hair is gray now.
When she was younger it hung black
like hay that had been coated in tar.
People would compliment
her hair & she would say
well, I am of Taino descent—

I remember asking her
I thought we were black?
She shuddered: *No, no,*
Dominicans only have Spanish blood,
Taino blood. No African blood, that's Ayiti
on the other side of the island.

History tells me
Tainos migrated
to the Caribbean from Venezuela,
I would like to ask them
but they are all gone now
like the eight track.
Someone just decided
they were obsolete,
replaced them with Africans.
Africans strong as earthenware
fragile too, made love
made a home,
brewed a revolution.

Still half the island
lives under white sheets,
speaks words like burning crosses.
Their skin, beautiful dark brown,
coffee bean, chocolate

They scrub
they wash
the trace of it.
Hold hand to breast
they wish
shade away.

The Day I Realized We Were Black

my brother Hector was four hours late coming home from work
when he entered the house   he was angry I was holding his pet
rabbit in my arms watching The Godfather — which part I can't remember
Did I mention he was angry   sixteen & angry?

& he said his legs ached like what a tumbleweed must feel against the wind
& he said he was tired like death seemed easy, like rice & beans
& whatever meat we had that night was too hard to swallow
& he said he wished we were white
& I stood up startled my much lighter skin than
his could not wrap my coarse hair around the idea that we were not that

because my mother is Cuban with grey eyes
because my father had an afro once but I had not noticed then
because my grandfather once said *I wish I were King Kong so*
                    I could destroy Harlem & those
                    fucking black cockroaches
because my godparents were Irish-American
because I had suppressed my blackness
because my brother shook me when I told him he was stupid: we were Latino
because he had missed his Jersey to Port Authority bus
because he was walking to the nearest train station & lost his way
because he was stopped by the police
because he was hit with a stick
because he was never given the right directions even though he begged
because trash was thrown at him from the police cruiser's window as he walked
because he was never the same
because we're black
because we're black & I never knew   I was twenty-two

Tio Monte

He was black as cat hair
always wore white linen
a wooden doll on a single brown
string hung from his neck
he told me he had visited
the other side & it was nothing
to write home about
a lot of lounging
not many beautiful women.
He did say once
he plucked a daisy from the field
it died quickly as though no one
on the other side was allowed
to own nature.
He would sit me atop
his shoulders when he visited
would walk me down
the street that way so I could see
to forever.
He bought me lollipops
saying they were the only right
thing left in this world.
& he would hum an old ballad
about a woman.
If I were a really good girl
he would buy me a flower
from the corner market
they never die when you pay for them
he'd say
don't know why they never die that way—

Tia Zulma

I curl my toes in the sand you keep by the door.
I enter & exit between our worlds that linger
discreetly: behind the ears, forced in my veins,
orbiting my bellybutton,

while you hold a semi-empty coffee cup
ready to see me engraved in the grains
left from your morning routine.

The white dress I would never wear.
The accident prone father I would never know.

Hungry, I would devour your smell of *menta*
& the residue of a relaxer applied meticulously
to your hair the day before: *to pull out the damn kinks*
you would say—

But I never saw the kinks, I only saw the foam
of blonde that encircled your face,
so much like mine, same wash of sepia overcast,

same red mark on the forehead,
but mine was a birthmark & yours self-inflicted.

When you peered into that third eye of mine
a trance would ensue, & you would talk in tongues
take off your white underwear,
drop them in a stock pot & cook them to know love.

Today the inside of my cheeks taste of the plastic
virgin on my tongue as you begged once
Bless her, bless her, she is your sister

That is the last thing I remember of you.
I do wonder if you still think of me.

I do wonder if I still hold magic over you,
& if the sand still lingers in your entryway.

Haiku for Iris

Iridescent you.
Purple petals. Your love so
tender, a whisper.

Ode To My Purple Dress

I made you up.
You were a dream, a Prince album
wrapping me in all the swaying motion
of twined lavender

You grape jam spilling
like lava over my volcanic body
dripping with you, how you
cling, how you swing & me
walking   taller

You, that one sunset I once
spotted over Mexico City,
how the sky burned around
your glow like begonias surrounded
by clementines. Tell me how you came
to be real, did I really just pick you up
from a sales rack?

You underappreciated jar of sea urchin

You Grecian vase covered
in butterflies like the fluttering
of orchid leaves on a humid sky

I'd love you, you really would
be the best purple thing I ever
owned next to purple haze,
I would love you, I swear except
this, you fine ass aubergine.
Your color in a certain light

reminds me of   bruises.

My Father's 50th Birthday

Us kids, we took you dancing.
We bought you just one drink,
a Long Island Ice Tea. You hit
on women our age; you danced
to songs you never heard.

It was a good night.

We forgot two years of jail visits.
Polaroids with white walls.
We forgot crack & shame.
We carried you out of the club,
you threw up on us with abandon.

Carried you like a dead body into
the narrow building, up the stairs
through the door. We removed your
shoes & lifted you onto the bed
to not wake your tired mother.

As we left we heard you cry out
Mami & at that moment you
were five & we were fifty.

We felt our childhood scratch
the back of our necks to let us know

it was finally gone   for good.

Needles

As a child I ran from them, pants
down in the doctor's office until
a nurse with hair wild as mint
leaves would hold me down, my
limbs like strawberry stems
stiff, green from nausea, terrified.

I've never liked needles
the knitting of them on a Sunday
afternoon, rain hitting my window
pane, my mother in a mood, my
daddy wasn't coming home today.

They were scattered throughout
our home; I would play
kingdoms with them, red ones
were females, blue ones boys.
There was always a dance until I got
pricked one day, & I never played again.

I've dreamt I never knew of them,
the way they'd lie on kitchen tables
waiting to be used by fathers &
mothers.

The way they glistened
sometimes against the poverty of
moldy bread.

The way my father
grunted with pleasure as they
dangled against his arm like a dancer
with tiny shoes on.

The way they rolled
down his brown arm.

The way they made him stare,
the way he stared—

Central Park Woods

Spam sandwiches, fishing poles,
& sleeping bags rotated around his head
like a carousel. Handling our little hands
he pranced while the pick kept his afro primed.

We walked the ten minutes past concrete
buildings & grandma's yani-cakes
picked one up on the way for good measure,
dad, my brother & I hopeful of a bear sighting.

We set camp by the pond on 103rd
because it was smaller & less likely to be depleted
of the great golds & crayfish.

My father would sit us on a sturdy rock
open a can of biscuit dough
to bait the rusty hooks
older than his affliction.

In 1984 my father took us camping.
He would cast the line across the pond
it would jump & form a wake created by his shaky hands
that longed for something else,
something foggy & familiar.

After a few hours we would
pack up our catch & head home.
Dad no longer restless
having found release from his day in the woods.

My father loved camping in Central Park
he would gather all the necessary supplies:
bermuda shorts for motion control
knee-high tube socks for barrier against the shrubs
an afro pick to keep the bugs out,
ache against childhoods gone by,
& a crack pipe to forget.

I Shook His Hand
        for Manya

before I knew
that in one eye
you were a child
pig-tailed, blue
dress, lace trim

in the other eye
you were a
roundness
he touched
at night

in the day
when no one
could see he would
offer you white
powder, nose
rip-ripe made
you haze

as you took him
in your mouth
called him
daddy & he
was your daddy
& I shook
his hand one day

I have a
picture of our
meeting, our
graduation.

He held my
hand & I
shook it

before I knew
he used to
tilt whenever you
walked by, doll in hand
thumb in mouth.

That Summer

Felt like a cauldron of sewer water
had been set to boil under
the concrete of our city streets.

Double-dutch was not an option.
The electrical wire we used as rope
melted a little as it kissed the sidewalk.

The white rubber casing would get stuck to iron
fences outside tenement buildings
to our jelly sandals
to our hair
like gum.

That Summer Elvis got his head blown
like a puzzle
in his own car
by his own people
for his own money.

My momma dreamt he placed a dollar in her hand
she played his birthday & won the numbers,

with the winnings she bought me a party dress
with lace & beading, it made my skin itch
but I wore it to sit on the stoop, in the park,
at all the funerals she took me to that Summer.

It was the Summer Tito got shot in the bodega
my brother Hector was there,
we thought he was okay

but for days Hector thought he got shot too
& he was our beautiful Taino ghost.

He would leave the refrigerator door ajar
or let the beans burn.

40

The salad wilted when he walked by.

It was that Summer
I remember

we ordered a carton of mangoes from our Dominican bodegero,
we ate them in silence as we fished & lamented by the riverside.

II. The City

What I
daydream about
the highest heels sharp
as steak knives
clacking against
city streets
like a jack hammer
on the road
to Oz.

Sappho in New York

I.

She was first spotted on the corner
of 125th & Lenox
her plaited hair curled. Her eyes
pearls through a rainy mist.
The incense vendor told everyone
she lingered by her table
preferred the smell of myrrh &
frankincense. She smelled of the
other side: wooden boat oars &
sleep. She carried a bag full of
poetry books & a purse
of the softest leather dyed pink,
rumors trailing behind her.

I first saw her on the L train.
She sat across from me, braided
leather sandals & her t-shirt
read "I love Ferrymen" & her
lips were crescent shaped
like the moon during my cycle.
Her arms folded across her body
to protect. She asked where
I bought my shoes, the leopard
print ones with the red heels. I
answered Jersey, she had
never been, only travels island to island:
Cuba, Dominican Republic, the Maldives,
Madagascar, Easter, Martinique, Lesbos.

My sister called on a March day
I saw Sappho, she said, *I saw her*
She was waiting for the M4 bus.
I followed her, I couldn't help it,
the rumors of her beauty are true.

She carried a lyre, her fingers,
they were the color of burnt umber.
Do you think it is because of longing?
Is umber the color of loss?

II.

It is so yellow, the way the buildings
stand upright & cast concrete shadows
against speckled sidewalks. The museums
are full of the Gods. They look as though
they were stone, but I know they are watching,
waiting for me to enchant them.
I only want to pull the strings of this city.
I am done with immortals, they are too quiet.
I love the sound heels make against the streets.
I am falling in love all over the city, leaving
peacock feathers completely abandoned on carousels.
Poems falling out of my dress
I cannot contain them.

The women here need me, the news reports
sightings of me everywhere, but I am not,
only where I am needed.
On the subway women carry heavy loads.
On the pavement their weary feet leave marks
that only I can see, like lipstick
stains against dirty napkins in dark bars.

Sometimes I am recognized, but mostly, I am
like a blue jay everyone thinks is a sparrow.
I hear them talk about me, they say I am responsible
for the city's young girls' disinterest in boys. That
since I've arrived women are taking over industry
& men have fallen behind, a drop in men that
graduate from college. But I care nothing of
industry. I care about the way a moan sounds
in the ear before the chest feels the first pang
of surrender.

Tonight I will strap on the highest heels,
stretch my body as if I were
standing on stilts
standing on bricks
standing on the long backs—
Arabian horses. I will balance my song in
that space between the neck & the shoulder
blade. Announcing to every woman
that burnt umber
is the color of poetry—

Ode to the Dakota

Some days I sit on a splintery
park bench & watch you.
I know that three bricks in
from the corner of 72nd &
Central Park West holds your
memory. I dream of asking it
for all your secrets. I
dream of flight so I may
perch on one of your gables
like an old time cat burglar.

If I could be invisible I would
slide past the doorman
into the courtyard where once
horse drawn carriages stood.
The gardenias smelling like
my mother's childhood.

I think you so whimsical, Dakota
I am sure the wallpaper in your
lobby is scratch & sniff. Your
elevators lined with velvet &
gold flecks & small Picassos hang
across from the inspection forms.

How famous your inhabitants
but I only really care about two.
I hear they are great neighbors:
Yoko & Roberta. Apartments
filled with gifts they have given
one another like the teak bathmat
Yoko brought from Japan, now
in Roberta's guest bathroom. Or
that wild leopard print rug Yoko
keeps buried deep in her study.

When Roberta is jamming late
at night, I see Yoko, glass
to wall, ear to glass, the flack fat
falsetto like a songbird in a small cage.

When Roberta has forgotten loss
she places glass to wall, ear to glass
& listens to Yoko's late night cries
as she remembers his soft steady touch.

Which brings me to this, Dakota:
I know this is supposed to be an ode
but I cannot forgive you for that day.
Humanity is not very good at
sniffing out the rotten.
But you, with your half-lit balconies
your terracotta spandrels looking
like gods on Mount Olympus; you
watched John get shot—

I smell strawberries when I walk by you.
His death imprinted on your façade
I place glass to wall, ear to glass.

On the A Train

for Aracelis & Patrick

What I remember is he had no shoes
& four toes on each foot, so his feet
looked like hands in prayer.
They were beautiful even in their rotting
like a drug addict the day after the first 72 hours.
This glow like a river running over skin, like an
aviary in the middle of nowhere, juniper trees
on the horizon
& he called me *brother, spare some change*
gender didn't matter.
His smile like a lizard fat after a feast.
His locks like old vines singing.
His hands had only one finger pointing
to god knows   where.

Magnetic

There are no rolling hills in New York City.
It is a city not as cold as Berlin, nor romantic as Prague
yet the horses look blue against the night, they draw
steel carriages that would take flight if it were not for the magnetic pull.

I miss someone today, his name I can't remember.
I met him on a corner, 105th & West End
blonde hair & brown eyes, almonds in a porcelain bowl.

A pull under my feet beckoned me to go one
way. Instead I turned onto a crowded gargoyled street
there he was—the incredible likeness of his hair to fur.
His kiss rattled my earth.

I know this has been said a thousand times before:
the attraction is lost after the contact has been made.

We break; I fall against the sidewalk like a ceramic knick knack.
The almonds like round magnetic backings roll away looking to
attach themselves to another. I am fragments on the ground
& only when I blink am I seen, like broken glass on a city block.

White Noise

I am holding on like a tan, weathered & peeling.
My hands are not mine, they press the egos of men,
caress, while my ideas are completely undressed
by keg-bellied meeting junkies, a sea of suburban lifers.

I twist wires at work & my fingers taste like electrical
tape I try to wash away. Rub my hands with soap
& lavender, rub against steel, peel garlic to forget the labor,
the uses, the being used.

One more conference call, my head will crack like a pipe.
One more "quick question," my legs will unbend & walk
out into the city heat, leave everything,
sell poems for a dollar near Central Park.

I may get a job at Starbucks where my manager looks like Che
Guevara's ghost; grey curls from under a Cuban Revolutionary
Party beret. I will kiss him behind the counter & pretend
he is still young & angry, not an old man waiting to retire.

End of summer, I am holding on like a tan, weathered
& peeling. I want to live in service of one word today, hunger.
I want to live in service of one action today, poetry. Rub my hands
with soap & lavender, rub against steel, peel garlic
to forget the labor, the uses, the being used

the white noise.

The Clothing & Shoe Drop Box

that resides on the corner of Madison & 57th is full of beautiful
baubles. I once saw an evening purse that resembled a dragonfly
encrusted in jewels. Not even the sultan of Brunei could have
imagined —Last spring I found a brand new lipstick, the label:
red like a burning jesus or vermillionaire. I have found silverware
with handles of bamboo, a shawl of grey fox, & a pair of platforms
from 1974, my birth year, lucite-heeled with turquoise water
& goldfish once whirling about. What use are these to anybody?
What will I wear when my mortgage does not get paid?
How will I beg on the subway? —With crimson lips, a pet
wrap. My shoes hold two goldfish poets who read Eliot & Pound,
pointing out all the people almost like me: apparitions in a crowd.

The Funeral

The night his old man died, her lover cried. His weeping carried
throughout the house, even the turtle hid quietly behind a rock.
She had never heard him cry before, the sound was deafening.
The realization so startling; the lover was human, he felt pain.
After the lover left, & his warm grief-stricken footprints
were left behind in the narrow hallway she slept. Slept as if
trouble were sitting on her side, in that curve that lies between
her hip — her rib cage. In the city streets, she carried in her proud
silhouette the misery of someone who was being forced to feel,
but still felt nothing. Even strangers paid her condolences tipping
their hat in her wake as her shadow collected the sympathy
that trailed her, it flirted with it, kissed it, batted its eyes at it. She helped
her lover pick out a tie to bury the old man in. She watched him
meticulously touch from silk to polyester & back again, as if touching
would remedy loss. At the funeral, in front of the casket she wept,
not for the old man, but for her lover. The tears fell off her chin
& onto the silver tie, it left a mark & he was buried that way—

On the Subway

Rat scuttles across my Jimmy Choos
like a flying fish across a circus tightrope.

The Pink Box at the Bronx Zoo

We walk, arms connected. I think
we are infinity.

You say *I would be an animal*
here, if I could get fed daily.

You say, *I am tired of it all,*
I would prance around for
someone's enjoyment.

I turn to tell you we   are
all animals.   I promise,
if I wanted to   I could
grow a tail or a unicorn's horn.

Before my eyes you are a lion
You   eat
my entrañas.   I let you.

The world is a curved face
your heart a shapeless bird
I want to clip your wings.

As you eat, you weep.
As I am eaten I weep too—

Notorious

It's all good *baby baby*.
But since you've left this
earth, taken your big-ass
voice away, I have been thinking
I never knew you.
But your voice, I knew it
the way it wandered through
my window late night, my hips
shaking from the fever it caused.
The way like marshmallows
the tender inside could be pulled
& melted, contained between two
graham crackers like a chocolate
silver dollar or a vinyl record
black as a shiny afro
on top of the man I loved.
Your voice glamorously
dangerous like champagne
on any other day but
New Year's Eve, like a June Jordan
New Year's Eve or a Neruda poem,
a Picasso painting, the square of a

woman's back never looked
so lovely as when you rapped
about it. & so my conflict
Biggie, is that had you passed me
in the street, you would've looked
at my tits first, before noticing that
my eyes, in a certain light look like
raw honey swirling. That you would
look at my ass even, & it not being
round enough for you, you would've
said something, hurtful, & I would
have hurt you back & then, you
maybe would've called me a bitch or a
ho & you would never know that

I could write a poem about you.
This poem would crack you
like an expensive vase
the day after purchase.
My words could be taffy or knife.
My words could be drizzle or downpour.
My words could be a rap song or poetry.

I chose poetry
& even with all I just said
I wish you were here.
I wish to give you the choice of
poem or rap song, & pray
you choose rap,
for nothing more perfectly
fucked up than the way
you presented the world
through your fat lips.
Nothing more real than
the way you talked about
women, as though you didn't

know them
love them
or late at night maybe
dreamed of
what it must feel like
to be truly interested in how
the curve of a woman's breast
can be shaped like an urn &
can hold you down when
the streets & the projects
& the crack vials & the
dime bags all seem to be
following you
home.

Maritza Called & Told Me to Write a Poem
about Michael Jackson

I could have been that girl
bruised skin from not being loved
thin, frail, sprite, soft-spoken even
except on stage
on stage I'd be fierce.

I could have sold the world
a fucking good day.
Thank me for your
courage, I gave it to yah.
Thank me for your babies
I gave em to yah.
Thank me for wanting to be
like no one else, see
I gave you that too.

I could have been that girl
who wore black penny loafers
that rode around white
iridescent socks
fuck man
I could have been the king of pop.

I could have been that girl
leopard spots right under
the epidermis, mating call
rub me rituals, HEAT!
Who closed her eyes
the first time & never
opened them.

I could have been that girl
hair kept long for tugging
mouth sliver slightly open
just in case one came along
& needed to penetrate

accessibility is an instrument

That girl who
fucked in her sleep
turned over &
prayed for a shearling coat,

hot pink
the inside of Michael's lips when he bit
too hard on the world &
the world bit back.

I Forgive Michael Jackson
                    after Propofol

The smallness of things   &   how we dare
to emulate   make ourselves   invisible
our hearts   hard-boiled   &   from it   sap
still leaks   a dam   or a poet   lost
to everything   but ourselves   & even still
this   massive universe   melted down   to a moment
of sleep   & maybe it's too late   for us
          maybe we are too big

our life is wrapped in a sliver the size of a needle

our love is the sound of   a   drip

& when we wake all we want is mud & dirt
& a wild   milk
                    falling
                              falling
                                        from our mouths.

Watching Porn with Angels

My sister tells me she will be taking
her students to New Orleans
so they can help rebuild.
There is a fundraiser at the Children's
Museum the students will attend.

Their job:
to interact
to talk about it
to sell this trip.

How excited
they are to fly
for the first time
to discuss the racial &
economic implications
that forced
the levees to break.

But how about the South Bronx,
where they are from?
Will they tell me how much
they wish to rebuild their bodega
so it carries organic foods?
Or their own beds, how the
posts are tied with twine & still
the frame leans left as they sleep.

In the vestibule three girls
hang on to me, tell me
they love my sister
they love the books she assigns
they love her boots, her face, her hair.

A woman comes up to us
says the most essential
aspect of all of New Orleans

is the cuisine, that they just need
to eat one beignet & they'll die
of delight.

The four of us stare her down
it is like watching porn with angels.
We imagine her bringing
the fritter to her mouth, the sugar
falling off the hot dough
spreading across the projects like
a dream. We imagine even

the whiteness of the confectioners.
the whiteness of her curving smile.

As if beignets are all that little
girls, brown & from the Bronx
go to New Orleans for.

As if all they can offer New Orleans
is a nod to their beignets

& then the moment is over
so quickly—

We then dream of buying
a million of those fluffy morsels
like down pillows made sweet

of releasing them like birds
onto the city streets
so that all the people
may eat.

Haiku: Jazz Guitarist Makes Me Wet

In the darkest bar
his guitar a music box
three hands, twelve fingers.

To My Co-Workers Who Said I Am Incomplete Without A Baby
for Kojo & Mike

I want to love a grown up.
I want to believe in that possibility.

I want to trust that he can love me
without thinking I am only made for

mothering & fucking. I want to
believe people can love each other

without distractions or debt.
I want to look in his eyes & say *yes*.

What I mean is he will be enough.
When the moon's fat shadow is cast

across my back at nightfall,
when the sun's fingers extend

through my window at dawn, *yes*
love lives here, in the face of

late nights & drinking
of solitude & a quiet so eager

to please me, that it strokes
my temple like an alley cat's

secret sigh or a flamingo's
pink promiscuity in the low

waters. I want peace in this
one life, I want to not worry

about money or hunger. I want
to see every inch of this earth

because I am so small that I could
fit in the eye of a needle & this

may sound like too much telling
I beg you, read my poems they will

show you something about creation
& control. I am a solitary animal

I will break at the sight of tradition.
In silence's sweet embrace I love

the world most, so I make a
decorative box of my precious womb—

Scare

That morning
on the subway
when the fat man
caused me to gag
his skin smelling
of perspiration
something made with
curry, a dream dinner that
without his scent
would have been my
favorite plate of all time,
I knew I was having
a baby.

That night I dreamt of
diaperless babies
wrapped in poetry books
Butterfly's Burden—the
purple cover, wrapped
between plump legs
sorrowful sobs
wanting eyes
a need.

Next morning
I woke in sobs,
leaned into my lover,
cuddled into his stomach.
Acceptance maybe,
then a cramp blistered under
like an eraser on old papyrus.
It was the disappearance
of a life that would have been
could have been
magic—

Vanishing like god's soft
beard against the world's satin
pillow, all of it
evaporating
with each
red
trickle.

An Elegy for Marco

I swear   yesterday I laid in the short grass
& a dandelion stretched & sprung its sweet tentacles
across my nose, I saw your face, a thousand blooming
buds freckling your perfect sepia build, a man that I loved.
This earth & its constant dancing around the sun is a miracle
as was the sound of your voice singing *ribbons in the sky* & this
might just be a poem about regret, not loss, but I am going to
write it for you anyway. I can't seem to recall where I placed
my keys or who I love today as I daydream of you filling me up
like a water balloon & releasing me against the world
like sins or a dove. I can still feel your lips trailing my neck
like god's finger—

I might just fall in love with every song
you ever wrote & spend eternity
listening to them like a baby's heartbeat.

I might just call up the man I love   tell him that someday
a dandelion might spring   & I
don't want to catch a glimpse of his face in it too

without having tried.

III. The Otherworld

In the absence of laughter
the joke goes:
drown yourself in love.

Bop: To My Lover Yet To Be

I am falling in love all over this city
with perfectly airbrushed underwear
models on the side of buildings. Chiseled
tree barks for jaws, soft lion eyes & hands that work
like all my favorite devices: remote control,
lipstick shaped vibrator, coffee-maker, showerhead.

Lover man, oh, where can you be?

I thought I loved well-dressed men with cufflinks,
peacocks with Cartier money clips & pink silk ties
they would use to wrap my wrists in, but the other
day I came in my hand dreaming of a construction worker
with a moleskine in his pocket a pencil stump over his ear
a half sleeve tattoo of Whitman's face & I swear I
had multiple multitudes. I still don't know
if he'll be an electrician with beautiful feet, a time traveler.

Lover man, oh, where can you be?

Maybe I'll write a poem about loneliness
Have it for breakfast with a side of bacon.
Maybe I'll date a poet, with a Ginsberg beard,
spend hours sifting through that cotton candy—
Maybe I'll just max out one of my cards
buy a new pair of boots high as the freedom towers.

Lover man, oh, where can you be?

Conversation

We don't touch. Palms cupping face, shoulder
rubbing shoulder in dark corners, elevators, pantries.

You never pick lint off my top   I never
investigate a smudge on your tie. We just don't

do those things. We don't have sex we make
conversation. & they are glorious little miracles,

rabbits pulled out of black top hats, coins
from behind the ear, almost a stroke of the lobe,

almost contact as when a soft wind travels
through a paddock, the grasstop rocks, but the soil,

the wet & dirty bottom does not scatter or sway.
We don't have dinners, we have coffee, & carefully

pass paper cups between one another, walk around
each other for milk, you drop the sugar packet in my

hand. & you mention everything, everything
except that, never that. I even tell you I take birth

control pills like communion wafers each morn, fearful of children;
the sound of little feet may spellbind me & I'll lose my way.

You look at me as though you may want to hold me loosely,
the way a nest holds a sparrow before flight.

We don't make love we make conversation, even in sleep;
I catch myself whispering to you in my dreams

& you, you always answer.

Haiku at the Soho Grand
for Massimo

September your eyes
olive colored, dizzy like
heat, Italian hips—

Synthesis

If I were a dandelion, let you be
the wind scattering me across
the whales ancient song.

Oh man's heart, smooth as porcelain
let my body be a narrow opening
for your wondrous beat—

Querido, your eyelashes are silk
against my tattered body.
Be unwashed & flawed   for me.

Let's make a baby or bake a cake, blow
bubbles with our eyes closed.
Let's build a birds nest,

I'll teach you to fly
you'll feed me your beak & all the bruised
things I've forgotten to savor.

Pink Box in Love

Six days in a row I've thought of you, before my neighbor's cock
croons its early morning song. My hand a drill, slides under,
goes to work, a good employee. Sometimes you kiss me first with intent,
sometimes with hesitation, then what I like to call desperation.
Sometimes there is a hard wall which you use to pin me against
the beautiful creature that lives south of your waist. Sometimes a soft
hotel bed. I lose myself each time. None of this brings you closer to me.
They say everyone has at least fifteen fears[1]. I have four: so I keep clowns
& rats out of my Picassos of us, realize that I don't know you at all,
not the masculine curve of your hip bone, not the nerves of your tongue,
will they dance for me? The last six days, I've been fucking my own self,
breaking apart from the sheer weight of my breasts, pretending
like the rooster pretends to know time, but what can it know
about want? No more than I know about your hands on my thighs
or even this, your own fears that cause your absence—

---

1   Forget safety.
        Live where you fear to live.
        Destroy your reputation.
        Be notorious—Rumi

Iktsuarpok

Mazalatan, Mexico 2013

the shaman said   *be ready*
& I bought a new dress   black   a million ravens huddled

he said   *love affair*
& I opened wide a calendar   lunar phase & all

he said   *fire*
& it was a million hummingbirds with their human faces dancing

he said   *madness*
& here I sit waiting for the honey taste of it to drown me good

had the shaman said: *lifelong   humdrum   safety*—

I would've cast a net across the universe   wide as shoulders
I would've built myself a raft   sailed towards   fire & madness
with my raven dress marking everyday   with thunder

but the shaman did not say those things

instead he said   what I wanted   to hear
these days I stare out the window
these days I walk outside every hundred blinks

the wind on my neck like what his fingers might feel like
      if he ever gets here
some days I check the horizon   hand on my forehead blocking out

      the sun
some days I even wave   in hopes of hurrying him
along—

Ode to the Mouth

Late night dreamer.
Beggar. Two suctioning half moons
facing each other, touching like lovers.
Pleasure palace with a slick tiled roof,
walls like a jellyfish, small cave, home
of one lonely eel, pink lollipop.

Traveler, wanderlust, I love all the semi
precious gleaming stones that align
your insides. I love that in you it is always
rainy season, in you there is always room
for witness. Let me decorate your
seashell with blood red stain.
Let me leave traces of you on a singular
body, you stiff maker, flower chaser,
poem whisperer. The ear is your best friend,
to it you transfer all of your secrets.

Wordsmith, dirty word slinger,
linguist, tu dices amor & it is so.
In your varied forms I learn how a little
boat must feel against the current.
I want to set you free—

Imagine what you can do estranged
from the body. Would you fly little
beak? Would you drag your filthy
lips over mountain trails, through
town squares, into big cities, up
elevators, around rooms?

Would you? Devour everything,
everyone? Will you grow so big
that you could swallow the whole
world? Swallow it like an oyster,
gift horses & all. Would you
chew on it like tough meat?
Would you spit it out like gum?

Mating Rituals

I touch it, two inches below your armpit
expecting to exfoliate my fingers
against the rough but it is soft.
Similar to how my breasts
feel at that lunar phase
when nothing makes sense
not even you.

I find a small raise
in the savannah of your skin
a red mound, like an anthill or montones
that the Tainos built to plant yuca
a long time ago.
I massage it with the palm of my hand
it tickles.
What is it?
I say, *I don't know*
& this means nothing to you
but to me, it means *I don't know anything.*

I squeeze it the skin slightly
discolored
reds & yellows where only
browns used to be,
like rustic leather.

Using my two
manicured index fingers
my ballet-slipper-nail-polish attacks
the red bump till
out comes the finest hair.

Alone it stands
having gone through
a birthing process
wetness & blood around it.

I run to the bathroom
grab the tweezers & return to the bed   our bed
where we make love
& lie like lions do in the Serengeti.

I grab the hair between the steel
points & quickly yank
The hair is extracted.
I can see the entire follicle
I got all of it.

I show it to you
let the tweezers release
this single hair
upon your hand.
You blow it away
kiss my nose.
These are the unspoken

ceremonies   between us.

Contemplating Forever

Eternity is a wet dream trapped in an hour glass.
          How lonely that one muscle overextending

itself over & over like a translucent jelly fish in the dark
          waters. No matter the glory of the embrace, no matter

the way that skin against sweaty skin slips like a freshly
          caught fish or a dead frog. You tell me ride & I think

for how long? Love is more of a motion than emotion. I imagine
          the tongue, a coaster, both upside down & falling in one

sweeping gesture. What can we say about contemplating? Your
          eyes piercing a figure eight, eternally tattooed in my mouth.

It reminds me that once I thought about sliding ceaselessly against your
          body & today I don't remember what you

looked like in my most feral imaginings. What can we say
          about forever except that it cuts like a blade of grass

& makes you tinsel. Sometimes it taste like salt, blood, birthed
          things, and other times it's so sweet that your lips part hoping

for the syrupy dribble to never stop. & anyway, what does any of this
          have to do with the blood red moon

looking like a caverned heart hanging
          in the heavens?

Hiking in Cold Springs, NY with a Man I Don't Know

Today, the trees are stripping,
private dancers in dim bars,
bodies rattling against wind
like poles; & me, I am staring
at your face, so unfamiliar, your
jaw a highway I want to touch.

Today, the leaves have fallen,
clothing gathered by a bedside,
a trail of loosened covers leading
to nakedness & wanting. I barely
know your name & yet I think
I know why your eyes pierce
me like a sword or stars;
I react to your hand
on my waist,
you are a warrior.

Today, one step in front of
the other, here in the wilderness
far away from the city I love
& love to make love in with
sirens & salsa streaming through
my slight opened window. I want
to give my whole body away
to you, here, with the sound
of a brook slithering on by. Will
my body know how to move
under you to the sound of deer
meandering uncommon like gun
shots not even a distant din?

I say, forget all that. My body
& your body are what the universe
intended when it made us. I say
we are not trees, with branches
extended like fingers towards the

other, hoping that a slight breeze
may service our need for touch.
We are the leaves, falling, falling
one on top of the other, whirling,
our veins & tips & blades like dusk
on sky. The earth is a solemn
grave & sometimes laying in the dirt
with a stranger, face serenading the sun
is all we can do to feel alive—

Self-Portrait as The Pink Box

They call me boxy, slightly round
edged. A vessel for trinkets & tongues.

They say I'm cute, sassy & sometimes
so beautiful, they consider loving me
in the morning light.

They expect that each time I open
there are miracles, poems & plenty
of love-making.

But my borders are fraying
& each year my heart sinks lower.

I was supposed to house a whole city
a million lovers & maybe a poem or two
in my honor.

Yet lately I can't remember whether
I'm a fishing boat praying for one catch
or a wild dog howling at the moon.

These days I barely recall what
it felt like to be touched by the man

I loved, or how like a tent my body
would unfold at the sight of him.

Instead I fill myself up with hands
& mouths that cause flooding & wipe
out what I've built.

This pink box is feeling so frail, lid
loose, he opens me without
permission.

There are no deposits here, no loose
change. Every so often he says: *I love you*
& it's as though he's taken all my poems

between his fingers. How wasteful,
to empty me this way—

Meditations on Beauty

Being beautiful is like being fine china
Being fine china is like being on a shelf
Being on a shelf is like being expired
Being expired is like being sour milk
Being sour milk is like being leche cortada
Being leche cortada is like being infinitely sweet
Being infinitely sweet is like being in love
Being in love is like being two people
Being two people is like being fat
Being fat is like being a crackhead
Being a crackhead is like being out of control
Being out of control is like being gluttonous
Being gluttonous is like being unfaithful
Being unfaithful is like being a liar
Being a liar is like being in control
Being in control is like being a dictator
Being a dictator is like being a forest fire
Being a forest fire is like being a path maker
Being a path maker is like being a risk taker
Being a risk taker is like being in the dark
Being in the dark is like being the other woman
Being the other woman is like being a catcall
Being a catcall is like being deliberate
Being deliberate is like being nostalgic
Being nostalgic is like being imaginative
Being imaginative is like being a fable
Being a fable is like being a poet
Being a poet is like being a lover
Being a lover is like being never satisfied
Being never satisfied is like being an over spender
Being an over spender is like being lace panties
Being lace panties is like being desired
Being desire is like being a stare
Being a stare is like being a kiss
Being a kiss is like being a suckle
Being a suckle is like being an orgasm
Being an orgasm is like being a mystery

Being a mystery is like being in hiding
Being in hiding is like being forgotten
Being forgotten is like being unimportant
Being unimportant is like changing of the guards
Being changing of the guards is like being brass buttons
Being brass buttons is like being a crown
Being a crown is like being a queen
Being a queen is like being brokenhearted
Being brokenhearted is like being dead
Being dead is like being nothing
Being nothing is like being beautiful and so on—

Saudade

I danced with your shadow
& love was made, like water
hitting smooth stone as it
tumbled from high above
& you were albatross &
you were a burning fire
a hand with fingers spread
like continents against
my abdomen & you were
ships sailing down a wide
shore & desire is a monster
with sharp teeth & your
feet were rocky temples
& I worshiped there &
I said *this is not loving*
this is no love poem. I am
devoted to a silhouette, you
wraith, you specter, you
ghost of a man, bearded
& uncomely. I thought one
day I could say *hallelujah*
but instead I am whispering
saudade, saudade reading
your poems & the words
are now tongues. & let me
be frank, I've kissed others
last week another man's
lips tasted of malta con leche
condensada, sweet hurricane
& my mouth lingered, as
his adoration fattened me
up, every stroke an eraser
wiping a blackboard & I am
clean again, brand new, shiny
for one moment, before
your face the moon behind
the clouds at midnight; an

apparition. I am sick of
missing you, I am sick of
re-living last year's fervor.
Passion is a wormhole &
yearning is a nasty demon
that dirts up your house
when you are sleeping
& loveless is equivalent
to torture & I am tired
of making myself promises
I can't keep, because last night
after spending a day
thinking I was done doting
on you. I fell asleep
& your touch was a soft
pillow over my face.
The future is an ice box,
madness is all that remains
& this poem is not the last one—

No More Love Poems
          for Brett Haymaker

I am not going to write anymore love poems
What's the use? You're not biting. My metaphors
are weak and anyway, you throw away
my images as though they were a sneeze.

No more love poems. When I look at
you as though you were a newborn,
& you insist on calling me *sister*
instead of *love*   or *baby*.

I am not going to write anymore love poems
instead I'll write political ones about my body
because my body is the most political
thing I own.

No more love poems, when I had to sit
next to Joy Harjo and hear her say, *please*
please, I fear for my life.

Not one more, because on any given night
while I touch myself to sleep thinking
of you families in Gaza are being dragged
from their beds, thrown in the dirt & executed
without a last look at each other's faces in moonlight.

Because 238 girls went missing   & still
Because imaginary borders
Because Chicago is a war zone
Because Jordan
Because Trayvon
Because Eric
Because Michael
Because Ferguson is on   fire   & I can't watch the world burn
while I dream about lions at the zoo.

No more love poems because shouldn't love for all
be a condition of peace?

Not one more
Because in my world:
We kill each other—

Acknowledgments:

Appreciation to the following journals for publishing the following poems:

"They Say"—published in *Chapbook For The Crowns Of Your Heads*

"Notorious"—Appeared in 5 AM. Journal Issue # 35 July 2012 & Nominated for a Pushcart Prize

"Scare"—Appeared in Adanna Literary Journal July 2012

"I Shook His Hand" —Appeared in OVS Literary Magazine Summer 2013

"Mating Rituals"—Appeared in OVS Literary Magazine Summer 2013

"Ode to a Dominican Breakfast" & "The Day I Realized We Were Black"— Appeared in Wide Shore Literary Journal May 2014

"Ode to the Mouth" —Appeared in Luna Luna Magazine August 2014

Gratitude & Love

My Mentors:
Jan Heller Levi, Tina Chang, Anne Marie Macari, Gerald Stern, Jean Valentine, Joan Larkin, Judith Vollmer, Michael Waters, Ira Sadoff, Cornelius Eady, Evie Shockley, Ellen Dore Watson, Mihaela Moscaliuc, Rafael Campo, Lorna Dee Cervantes, Norma Elia Cantu, Carmen Tafolla, Jane Mead & Alicia Ostriker

My Blood:
Mi abuelito Polito gone 15 years now but who I know watches me still, Maritza Rodriguez, Hector Montilla Sr., Hector Montilla Jr., Maritza Montilla, Carlos Montilla, Jaylin Montilla, Jonah Montilla, Eric De Silva, Janette Figueroa, Carmelo Ostolaza, Iris Montilla-Afriye, William Afriye, Christopher Mitchell, Manny Rodriguez, Cary Rodriguez, Andrew Rodriguez, Joyce Hernandez, Reina Rodriguez, Luisa Montilla & all the Montilla clan who nourished me.

My Tribe:
Natalie Diaz, Ross Gay, Aracelis Girmay, John Murillo, Patrick Rosal, Cheryl Boyce Taylor, Janlori Goldman, Caits Meissner, JP Howard, E.J. Antonio, Ed Toney, Rich Villar, Mahogany Browne, Idrissa Simonds, Charleen McClure, Charan Morris, Jayson Smith, Kathy Engel, Alexis De Veaux, Marta Lucia Vargas, Monica Hand, Lisa Wujonovich, Ysabel Y. Gonzalez, Amber Atiya, Clelia Mogolofsky, Michael Lee, Kevin Carter, Nirav Gadhia, Darrin Avila, Cindia Quintana, Denelle Burns, Phyllis Heyward, Kojo Ahenkorah, Shawn Hawkins, Milton Andrews, Demetrius Lemons, Esther Louise, Kerry Ann Williams, Azenath Adede, Lynda Sutherland, Rebecca Gayle Howell, Desiree Bailey, Laurie Ann Guerrero, Peggy Robles-Alvarado, Lupe Mendez, Eduardo Garbrieloff, Octavio Paz, Denice Frohman, Josephine Rocca, Cathy Linh Che, Mary Brancaccio, Marisa Frasca, Sosha Pinson, Darla Himeles, Lisa Alexander, Shaun Fletcher, Cara Armstrong & Michelle Bonfils

My Muses:
Lynne McEniry, Roberto Carlos Garcia, Sean Morrissey, Brett Haymaker, Heidi Sheridan & Peter Kirn, I hope we love each other this way always.

A huge huge shout out to Randall Horton for seeing me on the page & saying: YES!

Love to Joe Abate & Isabella Sessa who gave me Ravello, Italy & the space to complete this book.

To my Cravath Swaine & Moore, Drew University, CantoMundo & Cave Canem family; you sustain me.

About the Author

Yesenia Montilla is a New York City poet with Afro-Caribbean roots. Her poetry has appeared in the *Chapbook For The Crowns Of Your Head*, as well as the literary journals *5AM, Adanna, The Wide Shore* and others. A CantoMundo Fellow, she received her MFA from Drew University in Poetry and Poetry in Translation. *The Pink Box* is her first collection.